Stoicism:

Stoic Way of Life, Stoicism Philosophy & Wisdom. Create Life Long Habits of Mental Toughness, Self Discipline. Master Self Confidence. Control Your Emotions. Anger Management and Jelousy.

Table of Contents

Introduction..7

Chapter 1: What is Stoicism?..10

Chapter 2: The History of Stoicism...................24

Chapter 3: How to Become an Unbiased Thinker..32

Chapter 4: The Importance of Fortitude and Self-Control..39

Chapter 5: Using Stoicism to Become Free From Jealousy, Greed, and Anger...............................42

Chapter 6: How to Overcome Destructive Emotions..52

Chapter 7: How to Use Stoicism to Take On the Negativity In Your Life..59

Chapter 8: How to Recognize Stoicism in Your Modern Life..63

Chapter 9: The Stoic Methods to Helping Improve Your Modern Life................................73

Chapter 10: Why Should I Implement Stoicism in My Life?...86

Chapter 11: Is It Possible to Become Too Stoic?..98

Chapter 12: How to use Stoicism for the Long Term and Planning Your Future as a Stoic..103

Conclusion..116

© Copyright 2018 by Luke Caldwell - All rights reserved.

The follow eBook is reproduced below with the goal of providing information that is as accurate and reliable as possible. Regardless, purchasing this eBook can be seen as consent to the fact that both the publisher and the author of this book are in no way experts on the topics discussed within and that any recommendations or suggestions that are made herein are for entertainment purposes only. Professionals should be consulted as needed prior to undertaking any of the action endorsed herein.

This declaration is deemed fair and valid by both the American Bar Association and the Committee of Publishers Association and is legally binding throughout the United States.

Furthermore, the transmission, duplication or reproduction of any of the following work including specific information will be considered an illegal act irrespective of if it is done electronically or in print. This extends to creating a secondary or tertiary copy of the work or a recorded copy and is only allowed with express written consent from the Publisher. All additional right reserved.

The information in the following pages is broadly considered to be a truthful and accurate account of facts and as such any inattention, use or misuse of the information in question by the reader will render any resulting actions solely under their purview. There are no scenarios in which the publisher or the original author of this work can be in any fashion deemed liable for any hardship or damages that may befall them after undertaking information described herein.

Additionally, the information in the following pages is intended only for informational purposes and should thus be thought of as universal. As befitting its nature, it is presented without assurance regarding its prolonged validity or interim quality. Trademarks that are mentioned are done without written consent and can in no way be considered an endorsement from the trademark holder.

Introduction

Congratulations on downloading *Stoicism* and thank you for doing so.

The following chapters will discuss everything that you need to know in order to get started with Stoicism. Stoicism is a great philosophy to follow. It helps you to recognize more about your emotions and how they work, and ensures that you are able to maintain control, and choose when to express your emotions, and be the one in charge of your emotions. Most people choose to just let their emotions taking over, getting mad when things don't go their way. but this can lead to ruined relationships, missed opportunities, and so much more.

This guidebook is all about Stoicism and how you can implement this theology into your own life. We will take a look at some of the basics of Stoicism, the history that comes with Stoicism, and how you can use this ideology to help improve so much of your modern life. You can learn about how destructive emotions can get in the way of your happy life and how Stoicism can help you to learn more self-control, how to become an unbiased thinker, and how to use it to get rid of all the negativity that is already in your life.

There is a lot of miscommunication when it comes to working with Stoicism. Many people who have never taken a look through this school of thought think that Stoics have no emotions and are cold, but in reality, Stoics have the same emotions at others, they just choose to have full control over how they use those emotions, which leads to a much fuller and happier life. When you are ready to learn more about Stoicism and how you can use it to improve your life, make sure to read through this guidebook to learn how to get started.

There are plenty of books on this subject on the market, so thanks again for choosing this one! Every effort was made to ensure it is full of as much useful information as possible. Please enjoy!

Chapter 1: What is Stoicism?

Stoicism, or the stoic philosophy, may seem boring to a lot of people. Or perhaps you hear those words and think that it is a daunting task to even begin to understand what is going on with this school of thought. But in reality, the principles that come with Stoicism are pretty easy to work with and understand, and implementing them into our modern lives can help us to grow, improve, gain more control over our emotions, and so much more.

Stoicism is a way of life. It teaches you how you can keep a rational and calm mind, no matter what is going on around you. Many times, we feel that our lives are in turmoil. Things just aren't going our way. We think that everyone is constantly mad at us. We think that people are against us. We lose our temper, never get things done, and often feel like a failure in the process.

But with Stoicism, we learn to think about things in a different way. We learn that we can have control, and it is easier than we could imagine. For example, how many times have you let your emotions get the best of you? You got angry about something, frustrated, sad, or even happy, and just couldn't get the emotion to stop. You yelled and screamed, got in a fight, started throwing things, and felt like everything was out of your control.

This kind of thinking is very dangerous. It makes us feel in discord to other things that are going on around us, and can make us feel bad, anxious, and stressed out. Even though we may feel like we are out of control in this situation, we actually have all the control in the world.

In this guidebook, we are going to spend a lot of time looking at Stoicism and all the different parts that come with it. But one of the underlying ideas that are there is that we have control. Sure, an emotion does come up and we can't stop our feelings. But we can take a look at that emotion and logically think of how we want to react to it.

When we are angry, we don't have to lash out at others. We can acknowledge that the emotion is there, determine whether it is valid or not, and then decide how we want to react. Once you realize that you have all the power in the world over your life, things don't seem as chaotic or crazy any longer. Yes, you will still have emotions, but you will learn how to have control over them, rather than them having all the control over you.

Of course, this is just one of the ideas that come with Stoicism. Stoicism goes against some of the modern ideas that many of us hold dear. It realizes that there are a lot of things that are out of our control. We can't choose how people are going to treat us. Sometimes bad things do happen, no matter how hard we try to prevent them. But one constant that will always remain the same, one constant that we can rely on, is that we have the complete and total power and control over how we react to the world.

10 key principles of Stoicism

To help us get a better understanding of what a Stoic is like, and what principles are followed when it comes to this school of thought, we are going to take a look at the ten key beliefs that come with this. They include:

1. Live in agreement with nature and other things around you.

2. Live by virtue

3. Focus on what you are able to control, and then learn how to accept the things that you can't control.

4. Distinguish between good, bad, and indifferent things and adjust your reactions to those.

5. Take action. A true philosopher doesn't have to just sit back and let things happen. They are action takers and are even more effective because they are in control of which actions they use.

6. Practice misfortune. While Stoicism should be about learning to accept things you can't control, practicing a bit of misfortune can go a long way. it helps you to be prepared when things don't go your way, which can help you to really

progress because these bad things won't take you by surprise.

7. Add in a reserve clause to all your planned actions. Think of this as your plan B. The more prepared you are, the less minor setbacks are going to aggravate you.

8. Love everything that happens. No, everything may not be perfect like you want, but it is all part of the bigger picture of your life. Learn how to accept and love everything that happens to you, and you will get more richness out of life.

9. Turn all of your obstacles in life into opportunities. Often, perception is going to be key with this kind of philosophy.

10. Be mindful. Mindfulness is so important to getting the results that you want from Stoicism.

What does a Stoic look like?

The image that is usually out there about Stoics is that they are unemotional, unsympathetic, and that they don't really have feelings at all. While these people can remain calm in more situations than others, this doesn't mean that they don't have feelings. It simply means that they have found more effective ways to deal with their feelings. Instead of letting those feelings come out and make a scene or hurt someone else, they take control of the feelings and decide what will happen to them.

The misconception of an emotionless person comes from the idea that Stoics shouldn't allow themselves to be carried away by any unhealthy or irrational passions. Yes, they can feel these emotions, but they don't have to react to these emotions in a way that is unhealthy or will cause some harm to others. It is completely natural to feel these kinds of emotions, but that doesn't match with our rational human nature when we choose to act out just because we are having these emotions.

There are going to be times when emotions start to take over. Someone says something mean to you, you feel sad when a situation occurs, you feel overly happy and excited about something. These are all things that happen in our lives, and the automatic emotions that stem from them are completely normal. We can't always control was is going on around us, no matter how hard we try, and letting go of that and working on what we can control (which, in this case, is how we react to our emotional response), can make the difference between a Stoic and a non-Stoic.

In many cases, a Stoic is going to try to use training and reason to help themselves not act out just because they are feeling things. They don't ignore the feeling. But instead of just letting the emotion take over, they take a step back. They acknowledge that the emotion is there. Ignoring the emotion can be even worse than letting it out and letting it have control. So, as a Stoic, don't forget the important part of recognizing the emotion that you are having.

But instead of reacting, you will look at that emotion and respond to it with virtue and reasoning. After taking a step back, you may realize that you are having an emotional reaction, but in reality, it doesn't match up to the situation. For example, have you ever had a situation where you exploded at someone over something that was really small and didn't mean anything? A Stoic is less likely to have these situations occur because they take a step back, look at the emotion and the situation, realize that acting out really isn't warranted in this case, and then finds another way to deal with the situation.

Think of how many disagreements and arguments could be avoided if everyone was able to do this? It isn't always easy. The easiest path is to just let the emotion out and not think about the actions until everything is done and over with. But to add more calm and reasoning to your life, and to really make yourself happier overall.

The Stoic is not going to be someone who doesn't have any feelings. They have the same feelings that anyone else does. But they have learned how not to be enslaved to these feelings. This is not the same thing as being insensitive or without feelings. It takes a lot of time and energy to learn how to be more self-disciplined and to have courage. They have the same feelings as before, but managing these emotions and getting them to behave the way that you want, rather than you behaving the way your emotions want, is the key to gaining true happiness.

Think about how many friendships you have ruined over the years because you reacted in anger or in frustration, and did things that you weren't proud of. How many feelings did you hurt along the way? How many people have you driven away with your rage, your sadness, or any of the other emotions that you have felt? If you have ever done something and then later regretted it, then you have, at least in part, allowed yourself to be controlled by your emotions, rather than being the one who controls their own emotions.

Now, it is fine to react to your emotions at some points. This is the beauty of how Stoicism works. Just because you are following this ideology doesn't mean that you have to let everything hit you and you can never show happiness, sadness, anger, or any other emotion ever again. But the key here is that you get to choose when to show those emotions. If you take a step back and find that the situation warrants one of those emotions, then go ahead and show it outwardly. In other cases, you may find that the emotion just doesn't fit with the situation, or you may decide that, even though the situation warrants anger or another emotion, it just isn't worth your time and energy to focus on that.

There are many ways that you will be able to describe a Stoic, and these will really help others to understand more about what is in this philosophy. Some of the statements that help to describe the personality of someone who is a Stoic will include:

- They are confident and serene, no matter what comes their way. This does take some time and practice to master, so don't worry or get upset if you slip up on occasion.

- They act based on reason rather than on emotions.

- They focus on what they are able to control. And they don't worry about the things that they can't control.

- They accept their fate, without whining or moaning, and you never hear them complain.

- They are forgiving, generous, and kind. This often stems from the idea that they are able to control their emotions, and then they can take a look past their own issues and see the point of view of the other person in that situation.

- The actions they take are prudent and they take responsibility for them.

- They know how to remain calm, and have learned how to keep themselves from being attached to external things.

- They are going to possess a lot of admirable traits including self-discipline, courage, benevolence, justice, and even practical wisdom.

- They are able to live in a kind of harmony with everything that is around them. This harmony is going to extend into nature, to the rest of mankind, and to themselves.

While there are different ideas of what a Stoic is all about, many of these are misunderstandings of the whole philosophy. There are many benefits to this kind of ideology, and following it can lead you to inner peace, better relationships with others, and so much more. It takes time and some patience to learn how to keep those emotions under control, and as a beginner, you may slip up and let those emotions out. This doesn't mean that you are a bad person or that you have failed when it comes to Stoicism, it just means there is more work for improvement as you go on your journey.

Chapter 2: The History of Stoicism

Stoicism was formed in early Greece, by Zeno, around 300 B.C. The work stoicism comes from the Greek Stoa Poikile, which means "painted porch." At the time, this was a public space that was available outside where philosophers of Greece were able to gather together and spend time talking. Many theories were discussed here and many of those were then included in the initial development of stoicism.

Chrysippus was one of the earliest creators of the doctrine established with Stoicism, and he spent time expanding on these fundamentals in his own writing. His explanations of this early doctrine help to make Stoicism a very popular philosophical movement during his time, and even up to today. He is often given the credit of giving the ideology of Stoicism the acclaim and recognition that we know it has had throughout the years; all thanks to his publications at the time.

According to Chrysippus, everything that happens around us, including things in our lives and in nature, is going to be dependent on a specific cause. That is, if there is something bad that is going on in your life, there is going to be some root cause that led you to this fate. Nothing that occurs in life is going to happen without a sequential cause and effect. On the same note, he also believed that we each have a say and play a role in our final fate and that we hold all the power to change it. He believed that for an individual to have a free soul, humans needed to have a clear understanding of these patterns.

Up to that point, Greece had undergone many eras of philosophical thought, including skepticism and cynicism. Yes, besides their literal meanings in modern times, they were actually schools of thought that many followed in ancient Greece. On its own, you will find that Stoicism didn't really last very long in ancient Greece, but parts of it ended up influencing other types of philosophies and religion throughout the ages after that time.

While there were many ideas developed under the umbrella of Stoicism, the most important of these is that idea that we have complete power and control over our emotions, and the ability to overcome the most harmful and negative of emotions is the best key to living our best lives. If we give in to these emotions, we are likely to cause distraction and hurt in our paths. But if we can overcome those emotions, it is much easier to remain happy and to keep some of the close relationships that we rely on so much.

Training in this philosophy will focus on a mastering of emotions, which can give us the ability to react to the situations that occur to us in a logical and controlled manner. We each can have a life that is satisfying and productive, but first, we need to learn how to get rid of negative feelings and anger, and then replace those with more meaningful actions.

Understanding that life does have its own ebb and flow, that we all have things that are positive, and things that are negative, happen to us, and the ability to look at those situations both good and bad in a neutral manner is at the core of Stoicism and its ethical view. Remember, it's not all about failure to react to those things. You still have to be a part of the world around you and emotions are going to show up, no matter how hard you try. Instead, a Stoic realizes that they have the power to choose a logical reaction to any problems they encounter, rather than leading the situation with an emotional charge. It is a small difference, but it can really transform our paths and makes our thinking patterns change.

For example, you may get in a situation where your car breaks down and you are on the highway. You have a choice about how you can react. Some people may get upset and focus on how inconvenient this is and how they will be late for work. They get so caught up in the issue that they assume this is the only way to react in that situation. But in this situation, you have lost control. Your emotions are in control and you probably look and sound like a fool getting upset over a situation that is beyond your control. This negativity is going to carry with you throughout the remainder of the day, and can really put a damper on how you feel.

You also have the choice to take a view that is more Stoic. The car stopped working and now you are on the side of the road, yes, but it isn't something that you could control, and it really has no impact on you as a person. Being late won't end the world, and while this can be an inconvenience, it won't take long before you are able to get on with the rest of your day.

When you live in reason, it means that you need to have an understanding of where your place is in the universe, and why we are here. In Stoicism, the person needs to live within the laws of nature and then learn how suffering and negativity can sometimes be a part of our worldly existence. Choosing to passively accept this fact, and not letting it control us, can lead to a lot of happiness and contentment.

Another thing to realize here is that all things living in this world have been created equal and that this process is not just about ourselves. We need to respect and accept the virtue of others. We are not in this individually; we are all citizens of the world and can go through the same trials and issues, emotions and more as each other.

As you can see from this, Stoicism isn't just an ethical idea. It is a way to live your life. In essence, Stoicism is all about being in the present moment and understanding your part and your place in our universe. You get to learn how to control your life and control how much happiness you get to have from one day to the next. And having this control, though it takes a lot of time, dedication, and persistence, can be just the answer you were looking for when you got started with this ideology.

There are a lot of great reasons to accept Stoicism and the ideas that come with it. While many people assume it is just a school of thought that includes being unemotional and not caring about other people, this is not the way of a Stoic. In fact, they often get along better with other people because they recognize the other point of view, rather than just concentrating on their own. They are masters of their own emotions and know how to change the things they can control while accepting the things that they can't.

Chapter 3: How to Become an Unbiased Thinker

The first thing we are going to explore when it comes to Stoicism is how to become an unbiased thinker. Humans have developed a somewhat bad habit of putting their emotions, and all emotional thoughts, before any logical thinking. One of the main parts of being a good Stoic is that you will process your emotions, but you will choose to react to them logically instead. The emotions are still there, and the Stoic still recognizes these emotions, but the power they have over the individual is minimized.

Being able to do this and operate in a mode of total fairness is a virtue that most people lack in our modern world. A true Stoic is able to work within the laws of nature around them, and the idea of going against that in order to gain emotional status and personal gains is just going to lead you to a lot of problems later on. While it is in human nature to act selfishly and in our own benefit, this is a trait that can derail even the best of people.

Being unbiased in the thoughts that you have can really provide you with the ability that you need to see all the possibilities that are presented to you. People who only focus on the solution to a problem without considering the feelings that they have about the issue or those who don't consider who the person supplying the idea is will make the best decisions. They are able to think objectively and will take everything into consideration, without worrying about how they feel about the situation, or even how they feel about the other person.

We all have those people we just don't get along with. They rub us the wrong way, annoy us, or have done something that has harmed us in the past. But just because we don't like them doesn't mean they don't have good ideas to consider. If you pick out a winning project at work just because it was submitted by someone you got along with and ignored a project just because it was submitted by someone you don't like, then you are missing out on a lot of great opportunities along the way.

The brain is something that we need to explore a little bit here. The brain is going to process stimuli through touch, sound, and sight and then will send out a response. The first time that you gain exposure to something, it can take longer to process that information and make sense of what is going on. But the more that you are exposed to that same stimuli, the brain is going to start building pathways that can process the information faster. It will lead you to the same conclusion that was reached before.

This makes things easier on the body and is a matter of convenience for the brain. It is why we can do many tasks without even thinking about them. The downside to this though is that it becomes very easy to develop some negative patterns of thought. If we always have a negative outlook in situations, those pathways are going to become very strong, and we will always give a negative response. When you want to become a Stoic, you need to learn how to override these original pathways and exchange them for something that is much more positive.

Let's look at an example of this. Let's say that most of the time, you start to get frustrated and angry when you run into some traffic on the way to work. This can be frustrating, but not really that big of a deal. You have trained your brain to automatically get angry and anxious when you see traffic. This is a negative thought pattern, but it is primarily driven by emotions. You feel worried or angry about being late for work. If you take that emotion away though, then the traffic jam is just a matter of slowed progress towards your intended destination. It is no longer frustrating.

A great way to work on your brain and get it to change to a more positive way is to learn how to change the attitude you have towards things going on around you. Many of us can place ourselves as the victim in any situation, but in most cases, we are completely in charge of what happens, and we just need to see that. If you don't like the way that a situation is going, it is up to you to make the change. For example, instead of being upset about the way that your career is going and lashing out at your coworkers, you could decide to find a career that is more rewarding and make a change.

Taking the right responsibility for your own viewpoint and your own emotions can really become a motivating factor to make changes to better your own life. If you want something to become more positive for you, then you need to start treating your day, as well as those around you, exactly how you imagined in your daydreams. If you would never have a daydream about being rude to others and only doing the bare minimum each day, then you shouldn't let this negativity get into your day to day life.

Being unbiased in your life is not always easy. Each new situation that comes up is a new chance for you to stop and think about whether you are reacting on logic, or on your emotions. In the beginning, you will just react automatically, without thinking. But you need to learn how to remove yourself from a situation so that you can change this.

For example, if you are feeling upset with your partner, you may think that placing blame, saying mean things, and lashing out may feel good in the moment. But where has this gotten you in your past? Probably nothing but regret. Acting on emotions can bring out more bad emotions, and you get stuck in a vicious cycle that you can't improve. If you can't control the emotions, then it may be time to remove yourself for a bit, allowing yourself to think through your emotions before you say anything.

After a break, you may realize that the situation is not that big of a deal. Maybe you overreacted to something. Maybe you aren't feeling well. And maybe you were tired or hungry and that caused you to act a certain way. During this time, also consider how the other person views that same situation. Maybe they meant to say something nice, or something they thought was innocent, and your overreaction has left them confused and hurt.

Being able to step away from your emotions and think through the way that you react to different situations can go a long way in helping you to feel your very best. It can help you have more control, have more understanding with other people around you, and so much more.

Chapter 4: The Importance of Fortitude and Self-Control

The next thing that we need to take a look at is the importance of fortitude and self-control. Understanding how to navigate your own emotional response to different situations can take some self-control. It is something that you have to consciously think through, rather than just hoping that it happens. You need to feel your emotions, process those emotions, set these emotions aside, and then act in a logical manner when it is all done. The requirement to do this is a strong mind, and most people are not born with this skill. It is something that can be developed with a lot of training and practice.

In many situations, the idea of self-control is going to be seen as the same thing as being able to resist temptation. For many, this could be related to controlling bad habits, or food and overeating sweets. In the case of this book, it is more about resisting the temptation to act out on your emotions. Since most emotional reactions are going to be seen as overreactions, it is definitely a win in your corner if you are able to resist them.

Self-control is something that needs to be learned. While you may find a few areas of your life where you are good at self-control, there are some areas where you need to work on. For example, you may have a lot of dedication and discipline when it comes to the work that you do, but then you fail when it comes to the types and amounts of foods that you eat.

It is possible to build up more self-control in the areas that you want, as long as you are willing to put in the hard work to do it. The first step to doing this is to set goals that you would like to meet. No matter where you want to improve in your life, having a final destination, and steps to get there, is crucial. Half the battle with this self-discipline is knowing what needs to be done. We often procrastinate and spin our wheels when we don't already have a good plan of action in place. Once we have a good plan in place, it is easier to make sense of the problem so we can work on the issue.

Let's say that you have set a goal to be an unbiased thinker. You would set that as the final goal, and then you can develop smaller goals to help you get to that result. You can set the steps at what you would like, but make them clear and concise, set up a deadline for meeting each one, and don't' give up until you get there.

When you go through this process, make sure that you focus your energy on one goal at a time. If you try to work on two or more goals, you are going to find it is really hard to reach any goal at all. What you focus on is going to grow and change with you, so pick the goal that is the most important for you, and stick with that one until it is complete. Once you do that, you will be able to add on a new goal that you want to reach.

Chapter 5: Using Stoicism to Become Free From Jealousy, Greed, and Anger

Once you have worked on having unbiased thinking and you improve your self-control and your fortitude, it is time to move on to using Stoicism in order to become free from anger, greed, and jealousy. These feelings are seen as some of the worst kinds of human traits. These feelings often stem from feelings of inadequacy in your own mind. Many times we let our minds get carried away and we may imagine things that are strange or aren't really there. In reality, the buildup in your head hardly ever carries through when you look at it in your real life.

For example, jealousy is a negative emotion that can often be found when you are in a personal relationship. A partner who is insecure may start fights with their significant other to make themselves feel better. In the minds of this person, they imagine that a small habit, like getting back home from work a bit late, are going to be because of infidelity or other bad things, rather than just running late because of traffic or working late at the office.

The response of picking a fight over something that is pretty much nothing is due to what made-up scenario you were building up in your own mind. You feel upset and angry over something that never actually happened, in anticipation that the action did happen. This can cause a lot of problems in a relationship because the one partner has let their imagination, and their emotions, get the better of them and upset them, and the other partner feels confused and hurt because they are being accused of doing something they never did.

Instead of giving your imagination time to wander, you should consciously decide to think about things that are more positive. In the example above, instead of imagining that your partner is late because they are cheating on you, think about all the more likely, and reasonable, options for why they are late. If this isn't working, make a quick call to your partner and figure out why they are running late.

On the other hand, always giving people the benefit of the doubt can be a bad thing as well. For example, if your partner is always coming home late from the office because they are cheating on you, it is still important to trust your instincts. You don't want to set up negative ideas in your head where problems don't actually exist, but you also want to listen to your intuition and listen to those emotions if they are telling you that something is up.

This is the beauty of Stoicism. You are able to still feel emotions. But you get to look at them logically and decide if they are actually true or not and how you want to react. If you feel that your imagination is just getting away from you, then you can choose to put those fears away and move on. But if you look at those emotions and feel that something is wrong, it may be time to investigate a little bit, and then decide where to act from there.

Freeing yourself from these emotions can really do a lot when it comes to improving your relationships and making sure that everyone involved gets a better quality of life. Getting to the bottom of what is triggering these emotions in you is really the best way to stop those emotions in their tracks. Remember here that you are not ignoring your emotions here; instead, you are going to process and then react to all the emotions that you have in a more rational way.

In fact, the more emotional intelligence that you have in your life, the easier it will be for you to become a Stoic. The goal here is for you to not suppress the emotions. It is fine to feel the emotions, but don't let them take control over your life. Learning what your emotional triggers are and taking time to really assess what is going on inside of you can help you to have more control over not only your emotions but also other aspects of your life as a Stoic.

Now we are going to do a little exercise. Was there ever a time when you felt angry and upset over something that seemed pretty small. But you still created a huge response, one that was overreacting for the situation. Was it really that smaller thing that had set you off from the beginning, or was there a bigger trigger that happened in the background that then influenced that reaction in the small issue?

For example, maybe one day you see that your spouse left some peanut butter on the counter when they were done with making a sandwich.

Some days you walk by, put it back in the fridge, and that is the end of the story. But today, you get really angry and lash out. You aren't really angry about the peanut butter at this point. In fact, it may be because you had a bad day at work and feel underappreciated in your life. Or you may feel that it is a lack of care and consideration, one that you feel is a growing trend between the two of you in the relationship.

If you want to help yourself react in the proper way to situations around you, then you need to deal with the bigger and the original problem before it gets out of hand. This doesn't mean that you need to go through and rehash absolutely everything that occurred in your relationship since it first started. the better idea that you can work with is to point out things when they first come up. If you keep them bottled up inside, then it will be something small that will make you overreact to the situation.

And this is where Stoicism can come into play. When a situation occurs in your relationship that ends up making you mad or upset, then you will stop to think it through. You can decide if the issue is actually something to be upset about. If you think it is a big deal, you will talk to your partner about it right there and then. But if you decide that it is not a big deal, you will shrug it off and drop the topic right then and there.

This can be something that is hard for a lot of people to do. They will hold onto their emotions and the things that make them mad. They don't want to rock the boat and make things difficult. But then they ignore the problems so much that everything explodes over something that is small and meaningless. Using Stoicism to decide how to deal with all situations can make a big difference in how you deal with each situation.

Dealing with the problem that is actually bugging you, before it has a chance to become a big deal, is the best option. If you run into issues with this, consider speaking with a trained counselor to help you sort out the different emotions that you are feeling. Many of us can make it through much of our lives without addressing some of the problems that we face, so figuring out the best way to get started can seem almost impossible. Asking for help can be hard as well, but they help you to dig through those feelings so you get a better understanding of where they come from, and you can rationalize them, and solve them better.

Even if you don't take the time to visit with a trained professional, make sure that you learn how to openly communicate with others. Holding things in and never expressing your views and concerns makes things difficult in several ways. First, if you keep them locked up inside, you are going to feel bad about yourself, and something tiny will set you off. And if you keep those emotions inside, no one knows where you stand in life, and that can make relationships hard.

This communication can be helpful. The other people around you are not trying to cause you harm. They may not even realize that they are doing something that bothers you or something wrong until you let them know. They are too caught up in their own stuff that they don't realize that the actions they take are causing some issues and anger for others.

They don't mean this to be cruel to others; it is just the way that they got used to handling situations. Once you tell them that some actions are bugging them, they will be more than happy to make the changes. Just remember this communication is a two-way street and if they voice a concern with some of the actions that you do, be open and don't take them personally either.

This doesn't give you the right to criticize the other person endlessly. You can't be cruel about this. You need to open up the lines of communication and discuss your concerns with someone, but if you notice that they have had a bad day, or seem like something's going on with them, then maybe hold off your concerns. Don't bring up the concerns as a way to start a fight with the other person. Use it as a way to get your needs covered in a constructive manner.

Anger, greed, and jealousy can be the undoing of a lot of people and a lot of relationships. They are emotions that no one really wants to feel, because they can make us feel horrible and low. Learning when these emotions come up for us, how to avoid those emotions, and how you react to the emotions can really make a difference in how you feel and how healthy your relationships are. Stoicism is a great way to uncover the real reason that you are dealing with these emotions, and can help you to gain the control that you need over these negative emotions.

Chapter 6: How to Overcome Destructive Emotions

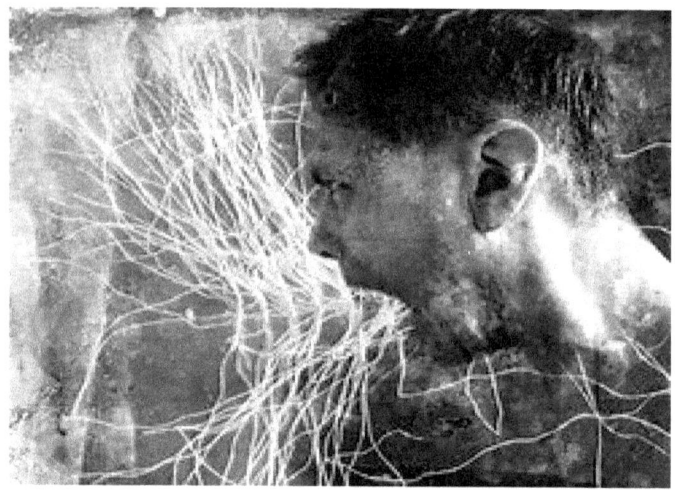

If you have ever allowed your emotions to take over the situation, you know how much this can get you into trouble. Those who have a short temper, even if it is only an occasional one, know that these overwhelming emotions can really cause them to act in a way that they are not proud of later on. They may say things that they don't mean, they may do actions they aren't happy with, and it can cause a lot of distrust and strain in every relationship.

In addition to causing issues with you and those around you, these feelings of anger and stress are going to affect your personal well-being. Jealousy and envy can often stem from feelings of inadequacy and low self-esteem. When we lack confidence in ourselves, we often have trouble controlling our emotions. We feel like we are out of control, we feel jealous of those who are confident in their own abilities, and all of this can cause us to feel angry.

When we feel in this manner, we continue to manifest even more anger, and more stress, that can be bad for us maintaining control, as well as for our health. Any emotion that causes us harm, and can cause to those around us, is destructive. But this is the reality that many people live with, and since they don't learn how to separate themselves from these emotions, they end up in a vicious cycle along the way.

If you want to implement Stoicism into your life, then you must learn that these destructive emotions have no place in your life. Not only are bad emotions like greed, envy, jealousy, and anger destructive, but too much happiness can be a problem as well. How can happiness be a destructive emotion? If you are happy but it turns you into a person who is inconsiderate and careless towards others, then happiness can become bad as well.

For example, if you own your business and there are a few employees who work with you, you must make sure that all of the actions that you take aren't going to affect the business in a negative manner. Being very happy and excited, and never asking for input from your team and from others before taking a new direction in your business can turn your actions into destructive ones.

Since happy destruction emotions aren't as likely as the other ones that we talk about, we are going to skip over these in this guidebook and will spend more time focusing on the negative ones. These negative emotions can lead to a lot of anxiety, depression, and stress in your own life, which can manifest itself in the relationships that you have as well. As a Stoic, it is important for you to learn how to get out of the mire and oppression of these thoughts so that you can remain in control and live a happy and productive life at the same time.

This can seem hard to do. We live in a world where it is normal for people to hold onto their emotions, pressing them down deep and ignoring them. But this never works. All that suppressing the emotions does is cause you to blow up at some little thing, and takes the control of your emotions out of your own hands. Stoicism goes against these ideas, allowing you to express these emotions in a safe and effective manner where you get to be in control and decide what is the best time and place to let the emotions out, or even to decide that the situation doesn't warrant the reaction at all.

A good method that you can use to bring in some balance to your destructive emotions is to find positive things that can counteract them.

Mindfulness can be used in this scenario. Learn how to be more aware of your surroundings, and concentrate on finding the good in life. Often we get too caught up in the negative things, the things that aren't going our way. But once we start looking for the good, it is amazing how much good will show up.

If you haven't already, starting daily meditation can be a good way to become more in touch and centered with the emotions that we have. Meditation allows you to take a breather from reality, to slow down and clear the mind, and it can basically make you wrap your arms around your feelings and thoughts with the goal of controlling and harnessing them. Even taking fifteen minutes during the day to sit alone in the quiet can do wonders to helping you when you first get started with Stoicism.

While you are doing your session of meditation, or even going through therapy if you choose that option, you should stop to focus on how your emotions have impacted your outside life. For example, if you are prone to bursts of anger, you can consider how they affect your job and those you work with, your relationships, and how successful you are in your life. Have you missed out on a lot of opportunities because of the attitude you have?

Many times, we assume that it is other people who are keeping us from success. We think that we miss out on things because someone doesn't like it, because life isn't fair, or because we have no control over the situation, but in reality, it is because those bursts of anger that you experience are turning you away from your coworkers and making it seem like you are not the right person for the job. The control is completely yours, you just need to learn how to deal with the anger and your other negative emotions to make this happen.

Being able to make the connections between this cause and effect is really at the heart of the Stoicism ideology. As the story goes, or the old adage, every action is going to have a reaction.

Each and every step that you have taken in the past is a result of the one that came before it. When you begin to recognize these patterns, and then work with making the right changes whenever you see a problem, is a great way to use Stoicism as a way to have more confidence and personal growth overall.

This process is going to take some time. You need to learn more about yourself, learn how to negate destructive emotional patterns, and learn how to control those emotions so that you can live your life based on logic, rather than your emotions, as much as possible.

Chapter 7: How to Use Stoicism to Take On the Negativity In Your Life

Stoicism can even be used to help you attack the negative things that are going on in your life. Many times negativity can seem to follow us around. No one wants to deal with it, but it is really a part of life that we need to deal with. We may not get the job that we want, those bills come due on occasion, and bad things happen no matter how hard we try to avoid them. Stoicism helps us to deal with these negative situations. You can't always control the situations that occur to you, but you can control how you react to those situations.

One of the best ways that you can attack any negative situation that occurs in your life is to imagine them in reality. In reality, you know that negativity is going to occur, and it is something that you will need to address. While some self-help books talk about how to just strike all those bad thoughts out of your life, this usually doesn't work, and it doesn't stop the bad stuff from happening.

With the theory of Stoicism, we are taught to imagine and logically think through the worst-case scenario. While it isn't the point for you to dwell and worry about every single bad thing that can happen to you in your life, but it does ask you to be prepared for them. When you are prepared for the bad stuff, or the negative things, you won't be taken by surprise when they, are something lesser, happen, you can remain in control over your emotions.

If you are able to take all of the different emotions out of a bad situation before it can even happen, you will find that you are better equipped to deal with that situation when it does actually happen. For example, have you ever had a time when you thought you would lose your job because you made one little mistake? The sense of fear and dread about losing your job can be crippling. But this won't happen if you already thought about it and prepared for the worst. It's likely that you won't lose your job at all, so you kept all of the emotions out of the mix and the situation.

In the scenario above, what will happen if you do lose your job over that small mistake? Would you be able to find a job right away? Would you have the option to go back to school? Do you have enough money to rely on or could find something to tide you over for a few months? Thinking through this helps you to get through a plan in the unlikely case that you would be fired for that small mistake. And often, you will find that things will be just fine if you do get fired. This can make even the worst case scenario look like not a big deal, and you can get through the situation better without worrying about the emotions getting in the way.

The reality in life is, there are a lot of events that can happen to you throughout your life, but very few of them are going to be life-threatening. The car breaking down, something needing to be fixed on the house, losing your job, and more won't kill you and won't be the end of the world unless you let them. Taking the time before they happen to look at how you will react in those situations can make a big difference in how the situation pans out for you.

Chapter 8: How to Recognize Stoicism in Your Modern Life

For many people, the idea of practicing Stoicism seems impossible. They think that this is an old idea, one that can only work in ancient Greece. They may not understand how this philosophy works and decide that it is too hard for them to learn and implement into their own lives. Or they worry that they will become too distant and cold if they decide to go with Stoicism, so they write this school of thought off.

Even though times have changed since the beginnings of Stoicism, and we are no longer in ancient Greece, there are still the same human conditions present in today's world as there were in the past. We as humans continue to grapple with the same fundamental questions including:

- How can I overcome the fears I have in life?

- What is the best way that I can handle any success and failure in my life?

- Is it possible for me to be a good person and help others, while still being successful?

- Why am I so afraid of death?

- When I feel like my emotions are trying to take over, how do I deal with them?

- I want to live a life that is good, but what does that actually mean?

The fundamentals that come with Stoicism can still be used today. In fact, since the basis of this school of thought includes good reasoning and realism, they can be even more relevant today than ever before. It can help you learn how to love others better, how to bear negative emotions, and how to gain more control over your own life.

In Stoicism, you learn how things actually work, rather than putting your own ideas on things and wishing them to work out the way that you want. This is where a lot of frustrations and anger in our modern world stem from. We want to be able to control everything. We want everything and every minute of our lives to fit perfectly together, and then, when life ends up going the way that it wants, rather than the way that we want it too, we become very frustrated.

When you learn that you don't have control over everything, you can then make your choices on how you want to react, and on the things that you can actually control. So, if you are anxious because you are waiting for things that may not even stay or arrive, things may not go the way that we want. There may be certain things that we can do to make them better, but there is always a bit of uncertainty, and we need to accept that.

Let's say that you want to have good health. You do have some control over some parts of your health. You can try to eat healthily and get plenty of exercise. You can make sure that you get outside and you spend time with others who are important to you. You can even go in for your yearly checkup to make sure that you are doing well. But still, there are going to be times when you will get sick, despite your best efforts. You may get sick less often than others, but you will still catch a cold or something along the way.

Getting upset about this fact is just going to make things worse. Everyone gets sick and worn down on occasion, and that is just a part of life. You can get upset and frustrated and lash out at people. Or you can just stock up your medicine cabinet, take a day off work to relax, and then move on with your day. Which one sounds like a better use of your time and effort and will make you feel happier in the end?

Another issue that Stoicism can help with is the idea of loneliness. When we look at this emotion from the viewpoint of a Stoic it is basically a feeling in need of any type of help that you lack.

It is a type of helplessness that has been combined with a sense of isolation.

This isn't how most of the world sees the idea of loneliness. We think of this emotion as arising when we are away from people more than we want or when we have lost connection to a close tie (such as when a close friend moves away or we lose a loved one), or even when an individual has some anxiety about the quality of their ties. But the Stoic definition can be more useful. There are many times when we are alone without other people and don't feel lonely, so the traditional definition can't be the right way.

If you let the feeling of loneliness take over, you may have trouble even living your modern life. Let's say that you meet a widow who often starts to feel lonely near the end of March because it was her husband who did all of the taxes. As a Stoic, she wouldn't focus on that emotion, even though it is fine to miss the husband. She would realize that using a tax software or an accountant could get the bills done and could fill the basic need that has caused the loneliness.

The widow is going to feel lonely because you think of taxes as a chore that makes her unhappy, one that she does not want to do because she doesn't need the reminder that her husband is no longer there. The procrastination that she goes through demonstrates a fantasy that she would be able to bring her husband back by pretending he isn't there. She may understand that getting the job done is the best choice and would probably make her feel better but she is determined that it won't make her feel less lonely.

When it comes to some of the thornier problems that we have to deal with during our lives, the remedy is simply to accept things that you can't solve with your own actions, and learn how to avoid the extra unhappiness of longing for the solution or the person who would be able to solve it for you. You should also be wary of berating yourself in this situation because you haven't brought in the right problem solver to make things better. This just makes the situation worse in the long run.

Loneliness is just one of the issues that you may have to deal with when it comes to Stoicism in our modern world. You want to be able to deal with all of the negative emotions, including longing, loneliness, anxiety, and anger. You may only have one or two of these that are really bad in your life, but it is still important to take the time to learn how to handle these strong emotions and not let them take control over you.

Overcoming these negative emotions is something that is going to take a lot of training. Think of mastering Stoicism like you would with mastering any other skill, such as a new instrument, doing something in math, or learning how to drive. You need to spend some time practicing and taking lessons, and you are going to make mistakes. But it does get better.

Stoicism can help you to find remedies for anger, and the other negative emotions, so that you are able to feel better and not have to worry about how they take control over your life. Let's take an example of anger. If you are dealing with anger on a regular basis, some of the steps that a Stoic may be able to use to help them deal with the anger and not let it take control over their lives will include the following:

- Engage in some meditation ahead of time to help you feel calmer and not let anger take control.

- Check anger as soon as the symptoms start to creep in. Never wait on this because anger can quickly get out of control.

- Try to avoid people who make you angry and irritable, and instead focus on ones who are serene and easier to get along with. The Stoic mind will be able to figure out who will fit best with them.

- Do some purposeful activity that can relax the mind and makes the stress and anger go away.

- Find environments that you can spend your time in that have pleasing colors.

- Don't try to engage in a deep conversation when you feel tired.

- Don't engage in these same deep conversations when you feel hungry or thirsty.

- Engage in cognitive distancing. This is basically when you learn how to delay your responses so that you can think through them and pick the right reactions for the situation.

This is just an example of how you can use a Stoic mind to help you deal with the anger that is going on. But you can employ these same steps if you are dealing with loneliness, frustration, sadness, or some other negative emotions. It is important to learn how to recognize those emotions and acknowledge that they are there. But from there, you can move on to thinking logically about how you want the situation to play out, how you want to look to other people, and so much more.

Chapter 9: The Stoic Methods to Helping Improve Your Modern Life

If you are looking for a guide that can help you keep all your sanity in our complicated and busy modern world, then Stoicism is the right choice for you. You may wonder why you would want to follow a school of thought that comes from the ancient Greeks, but anyone who has tried it out in the past and implemented it into their lives has found that it can be a great way for them to improve their lives, get a handle on their emotions, and so much more. Our modern world, perhaps more than any other time in history, really needs a steady framework to help them set priorities, orient themselves, and learn how to appreciate all the good in their life while handling all the bad.

While the ideas of Stoicism may seem complicated or like it is too old and ancient to apply to our modern lives. But in many ways, when you start to add these principles into your life on a daily basis, you will be surprised at how liberating it can feel.

When it comes to adding more Stoicism to your life, there are going to be four main virtues that are very important to seeing results. These include:

- Practical wisdom: This is the knowledge of what is bad and what is good, and what needs to be done in both cases.

- Courage: This isn't just talking about physical courage. It also is going to talk about moral courage or the courage that you need to face all of your challenges each day with integrity and clarity.

- Temperance: This is going to be the exercise of moderation and self-restraint in all the different aspects of your life.

- Justice: This is where you will work on treating others fairly, even if they have done you wrong.

At the base of this philosophy is the idea to respect other humans. The ancient Stoics were the only group of free people at that time who openly opposed slavery and who considered women to have the same rights as men. With that said, it is a great ideology to implement into your own life any time that you want to make improvements, or when you see that things just seem to be overwhelming to handle on your own.

In this chapter, we are going to take a look at some common modern challenges that many people tend to face, as well as the approach that you would use as a Stoic to help you handle that situation. As you go through, you will quickly see that this is a great method to add to your own life, that it is simple, and you will see results in no time.

I'm under stress all the time

Despite what it may feel sometimes, stress is not something that is placed on you. Often it becomes a part of your life because you have expectations that are misguided, you are attached to certain outcomes occurring, or you try to control things throughout your life that you can't control.

Let's say that you would like to finish getting a room prepared for your aging parents to move into, but you weren't able to get it done by the deadline that you implemented on yourself. You should accept that, rather than getting mad and wallowing in regret. Remember that you aren't able to always control the outcomes of situations. But you can also turn this into a good learning experience for setting more realistic expectations next time.

A practice that you can try out when you want to deal with this problem is to get out a journal and write out the answers to three important questions. These questions are - What could I have done differently today? What were some of the things that I did right today? What did I do wrong today?

I have demands that are really relentless on my time

A Stoic is often going to realize that their time is a very precious resource. And they refuse to easily give it away since they can never get that time back. They also know that they shouldn't fritter away their time on things that are not worth it. As a Stoic, it is important to learn when you should say no to people, especially when it is not something you want to do or something that you are comfortable with giving away.

In the same idea, make sure that you aren't stealing time away from the people who really do matter to you. Yes, you may have five hours available after work, but giving 4 away to one person may mean that you miss out on time with your family or those you love the most. As a Stoic, you need to place a strong emphasis on responsibility to your family so time taken from them is never a good thing and they avoid it as much as possible.

I end up spending a lot of time online, and then I feel bad

As a Stoic, you recognize that technology isn't a bad thing, but it isn't always a good thing either. The way that you use this technology is what is really under your control, and can help make you a better person. You don't have to give up technology and online time just because you are a Stoic. But if you are wasting time online, spreading gossip online, and using that instead of spending time with your family, then there is something wrong with the technology.

If you use your Stoic training in the proper way, you will find that digital technology can be like a virtue gym. It gives you a lot of opportunities to exercise your character and your ethics. When people say things that are mean to you or aggressive, you can choose to not respond to the issue. You can delete the post or unfollow instead if you can't ignore it, but avoiding a big confrontation can be the best way to make sure that you maintain your control over the situation without letting it get the best of you.

Even though I'm not doing horrible financially, I never feel content with my possessions and wealth

This is a big problem that many people in the modern world feel. They may make a good income, but we are often bombarded with a lot of advertisements and other media that show us glamorous lives. We see all the things that other people have, and we feel like we are falling behind. This emotion of envy and jealousy can rear its ugly head and make it very difficult to be happy with the things that we already have.

There is nothing about the ideology of Stoicism that says that wealth is bad or that you can't have wealth and use it to have a good life. The ancient Stoics came from all walks of life. Some were slaves and some were very rich. There is nothing wrong with money or having money, but Stoicism often sees it as a great temptation if you don't know how to use it properly. The more people have of wealth, the more they are going to focus on expensive experiences and possessions, and the more they will want.

How do you get yourself out of this endless cycle of getting more money, and then always wanting more? First, you need to recognize that possessions are just external objects, things that you can lose. Yes, they are nice to have and you are lucky to own them, but it is possible that your luck will turn at any moment, and then all those things will be gone.

Now, this is the worst case scenario, losing all your possessions. Now that you have been able to mentally accept this outcome, which is unlikely, you can learn how to change your mindset about the things that you own. If you run into issues with this one, you may want to try "practicing" not having things for a bit. This helps them to get used to the idea that everything they have is going to be borrowed from the universe, and you are lucky to have them.

When we learn how to appreciate the things that we have more, and we see them as gifts from the universe, some of that longing for more wealth, for more possessions, will go away. Sometimes it is all about removing some emotions, like envy and jealousy, from the situation to help you to appreciate what you have and keep yourself from worrying about material things.

As I age, I always feel worried about the health I have

All of us have health conditions when we get older, no matter how well we take care of ourselves along the way. While there are a few things that you can do to help improve your health, such as eating healthy, getting some social interactions rather than being isolated, visiting the doctor, and being physically active, aging can catch up with you. You can reduce the severity of it, but you will notice a difference between your 60-year-old body and your 40-year-old body.

In this scenario, it is important to recognize what you can control, and what you are not able to control. You should also learn how to let go of the desire to control outcomes in your life because these are definitely out of your control. You can avoid bad stuff, eat right, and exercise, and make the right medical decisions all day long, but you are still going to get sick on occasion, and you can't always control the outcome of that illness.

In a sense, when you worry too much about yourself and whether or not you will get sick, you are participating in a form of narcissism, an attitude that Stoics will want to avoid. You are able to avoid this by simply recognizing yourself about your place in space and time. in a world where focusing on yourself is seen as completely normal, this can take some time. and it isn't an invitation to forget about yourself and never take care of yourself. But it is a way for you to learn how to let go of various things, like getting a cold, that you aren't able to control.

I feel fear when I think about dying

No matter how scary it may seem to some people, death is natural, and it is something that is going to happen to everyone. We must accept this, or it is impossible to be truly happy as you live your life. If you are constantly fearing death and being worried about it, how are you supposed to enjoy the life that you have? You can't control death. It is going to come at any time and manner that it wants no matter what you have to say about it, and trying to force it to behave in any other way is futile. Accepting death and the afterlife can be a good way to find true happiness.

Part of accepting death is to prepare for it, but this is definitely not something that Americans work on. They never put together a will, they do not worry about a power of attorney, and they never put out a do not resuscitate order. This can make it very hard at the end of your life, both for you and for those who have to take care of you.

Stoics consider it a very courageous thing to prepare for death and the end of life, and it is a refreshing exercise. This exercise forces you to get through your fears, your anxiety, and even your anger so that you think in a rational manner. According to even the most ancient Stoics, the biggest test of character is how one handles the last moments of their life. Prepare for your end of life ahead of time, face your fears, and you will soon see how being a Stoic can benefit your life.

The examples that we discussed above are great ways to show how Stoicism, even though it is an ancient philosophy, can be used in our modern world. More than ever, our modern world has left people emotional, out of control, stressed out, and not sure what to do. Implementing the Stoic philosophy into your life and trying to follow it as much as possible may be the answer that you need to help solve many of the major problems you face today. Once you get past the misconception that Stoicism is all about being cold and heartless, you will see that it is actually a great approach that can help you to improve your life and see great benefits.

Chapter 10: Why Should I Implement Stoicism in My Life?

This guidebook has taken some time to talk about the various parts of Stoicism. We looked at the main principles that come with this ancient school of thought, why it is so important to the different parts of your life, and even some ideas on how you can start to implement it today. But now it is time to take a look at some of the basics of why you should implement Stoicism into your life, and the basics of why it can make great improvements in your life, even in our modern life.

Helps you build better relationships

One of the best benefits that you will be able to get when you get started with Stoicism is that it helps you to have better relationships with everyone around you. You get the benefit of having a better relationship with your family, with friends, with co-workers, and with other people you encounter each day. It may take some time to accomplish, but if you work at it, you are going to see a huge improvement in your overall quality of life and the types of relationships that you get to enjoy.

Think of how hard it is for other people to be around you. When you explode over little things or get too emotional and can't stop because the emotions have started to take over, you can be very unpredictable and hard to get along with. You may drive a lot of people away from you, people who don't really want to deal with all the emotions, or who were hurt along the way and decided to give up.

With Stoicism, you can change this. You can get in control of those emotions and tell them when you want them to come out. This doesn't mean that you aren't allowed to have any emotions at all. It simply means that you need to take a step back from the emotions, think about those emotions in an objective manner, decide if the situation warrants those emotions at all. If the situation does warrant the emotion, then you can express it. If the situation doesn't warrant that emotion, then you need to learn to just let it go and move on.

Helps you to not sweat the little things

Often the things that are the smallest are the ones that get us worked up the most. A glass left on the counter is a small deal, but many times we let it blow out of proportion and then get into a fight because that glass was left out. We worry about being a few minutes late to school. We worry about what we are wearing and if anyone will think that it looks bad. We worry about a million little things, and we let these things take over our lives, but none of them are really worth the effort.

With Stoicism, we start to take a look at our lives and our actions and make conscious decisions on how we want to react to things. We learn to let go of all the little things that we can't control. If you are late for work because you leave the house too late, then make a change and leave home a few minutes early. But if you are late for work once because there was an accident on the road that stopped all traffic, then just let it go.

You will be surprised at how many little things you hold onto and make into big deals once you start looking into them. Allowing these little things to control your emotions and cause problems is really not worth it. Use Stoicism to help you let go of the little things, to keep your emotions in check, and see how well your happiness can grow over time.

Helps you to be in more control over your life

Do you ever feel that you are losing out on the control that you want in your life? Do you feel that others get to make the decisions for you, or that your emotions are ruining all of your relationships? Then it is time to make some changes and Stoicism can make the results that you would like.

If your emotions have control over your life, it becomes really hard for you to get the things that you want. If a little bit of anger can make you overreact and then you do or say something that you don't mean, this can be really damaging in many aspects of your life. If these anger emotions cause you to be mean and say bad things to your partner, then you may find that they get tired and they leave. If you let these emotions come out when you are at work or other social situations, you could make it hard to make friends, to get along with others, and even keep your job.

When you start to implement the ideas of Stoicism into your own life, you will find that it is easier to get this control back. Remember that Stoicism doesn't mean that you have to be devoid of emotions. It just means that you decide when and how to use those emotions. If you take a look at an emotion and decide that it isn't the right one for that situation, or you decide that you don't want to waste your time on that emotion, then you will move on and handle the situation in a different way.

In some cases though, you may decide that it is best to let the emotion out. Stoics do feel anger at some points. But instead of letting it turn into all-out rage and letting it ruin how they interact with others, they use that anger to help tell someone what is bothering them or even to effect change in the world. A Stoic can easily be happy and joyous about something, but they learn how to manage it so that the emotion doesn't take over and make them into something bad. In Stoicism, there is even room for the other emotions, the Stoic is just more in control of them and can make the big decisions on when and how to use those emotions.

Can help you handle stress better

How many times do you feel the stress creep up on you? You feel that you are overwhelmed by what is going on in your life, you may want to scream and get angry, your neck muscles tighten and you may even catch your hands in a fist by your sides. Stress can cause so many issues to the body, such as an elevated heart rate, health conditions, headaches, and so much more. But despite these issues, you will find that most Americans are dealing with stress, at least part-time, and can't seem to make it go away.

Stress is often going to be a side effect of not being able to control what is going on around you. You want to have control, but you find that some things are just not going to work the way that you would like. In addition, it could be a result of issues of not being able to manage your time and say no to things that don't really mean much to you (such as helping out at work more when you'd rather spend time with your family), which can make us feel very stressful.

Stoicism can help you to deal with the stress in your life. You learn how to recognize the emotions that are going on in your mind, and then you can make decisions based on what will make you the happiest and will ensure that you get what you want out of life. When you can make smart decisions that make your life easier, and when you learn to let go of the things that you have no control over, you will find that the stress starts to go away.

Helps you to live in the present moment

How many times do you focus your energy on thinking about what happened in the past, or what is going to happen in the future? Now compare that time to how much time you actually spend concentrating on the here and now, the things that actually matter at this point in life. Often, the latter is only going to happen when a big, significant thing happens in our lives, but as a result, we are missing out on so much that can be amazing.

Stop focusing so much on the past and the future. You can't do anything about what happened in the past, and until someone creates a time machine and you can use it to go back, you just have to live with what occurred. And while you can make different decisions to help influence the future, you can't have full control over what is going to happen to you in the future either. So why get so worked up and worried about it, and why spend so much of your time focusing on it, when you could just focus your energy on the here and now and see some great results instead.

Helps you to stop caring what others think about you

It has happened to all of us. We worry about the way that others perceive us. We dress up a certain way because we think that it is important to have a certain appearance to different events. We worry that when we mess up, others are going to think lower of us and make fun of us, and this can cause a whole host of other issues along the way.

With Stoicism, you can learn how to not worry about these things as much. It may be hard. We live in a society where appearances seem to matter more than they should, and we all want to live up to an impossible standard that the celebrities like to shove on us. But this is not the way that most people live, and neither should you. It just adds in stress, brings out our own insecurities, and so much more.

Stoicism can help us to take a step back and not focus on what others think so much. Instead, you will learn more about how to take a step back, figure out why your appearance towards others is so important, and then make the changes necessary to free yourself from that idea and just enjoy life instead.

Learn how to be thankful for what you have

Often our emotions can make us feel ungrateful or sad about the things that we have. We may have a nice place to live, food on the table, and so much more, but we still feel like we are missing out or like we don't have the same things or quality of life that others do. This can make it hard to feel happy, and those feelings of anger, jealousy, and envy just keep getting worse.

When we are able to implement the ideas of Stoicism into our lives a bit more, we find that it is easier to be thankful for what we have. When we see that someone else has something nice, or something that we want. We can choose not to react and then take a step back and see all of the good things that we do have. And once we take a close look at all the blessings that we already have, it becomes a lot easier to be thankful.

Implementing Stoicism into your life is not always going to be easy. Humans can be very emotional creatures and turning those emotions off, or at least being able to control them and think about them critically is not something that we are used to. But the tips and tricks in this guidebook are there to help you along the way and will give you the guidance and help that is needed to really see Stoicism work for your needs.

Chapter 11: Is It Possible to Become Too Stoic?

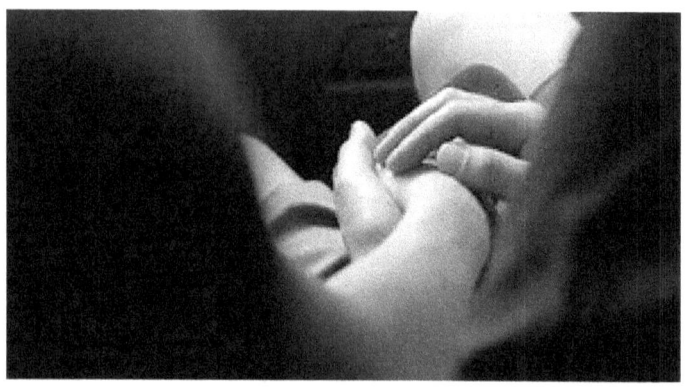

The next question that you may have about the ideology of Stoicism is whether it is possible to be an extreme Stoic? Is it possible to take this idea too far and become so Stoic that no one wants to be around you? If you are following the principles that the found fathers had with Stoicism, it isn't possible to take this to the extreme. With that said, Stoicism can sometimes be used in the improper manner and this has given it a rap as an emotionless existence where the person is overtly logical and cold and doesn't take the feelings of the other person into consideration.

When it comes to Stoicism, you will find that it can be the perfect combination of compassion and logic. You can still feel your emotions, you can still feel the plight of someone else, respect their boundaries, and the laws of nature and this earth, and still make decisions that are logical and ones that don't have emotions that control or drive them. While this doesn't seem like it to someone who hasn't practiced Stoicism, the emotions actually are a big part of the decision making process. You just decide in a logical manner if you are going to let the emotions play a part in your reaction or not.

Let's say that you are thinking about switching jobs. There are some benefits that come with working at your current job including a company car and a good benefits package that you already enjoy. Based on the idea of financial security, you really don't have a good case for leaving this position. However, in return for these benefits, you have a lot of long hours and stress for being there, and you feel pretty drained each day. This can negatively affect your relationships and even your ability to find some joy in life.

In many cases, an individual, even a Stoic one, would decide to leave their secure job and go for the other one if it had a decent pay, had good benefits, and promised fewer hours so they could enjoy life. These may not seem like logical choices when looking at finances, but the emotional considerations came into place with this decision.

If the Stoic were only about the logic of tangible things, such as their income, there would be one solution; stay where you are. But no one is able to ignore their emotions completely. In fact, feelings and emotions, specifically the stress response, are the way the body tells you that something is off and that you need to make some changes to your situation. Emotions don't have to be ignored in any situation, but you need to really consider them when making decisions, rather than letting them take over and control you.

Even as a Stoic, your decisions will be a balance of logical and emotional reason. A good compromise to work with would be to stick it out at the first job while looking around for a new place to work. This means that you are able to still receive your income and your benefits until you find something else that you will enjoy better.

If you start to lose connections with others, then you know that you have taken the idea of Stoicism too far. Thinking too logically means that you are going to take too much time away from some of the simple things that you should enjoy in life. And being too logical can make you seem cold and unsympathetic to those around you, driving relationships away. Stoicism should be a way to improve your relationships, not drive others away. If you feel that people are being driven away by the way that you act, then it is time to make some adjustments to what you are doing with Stoicism.

Chapter 12: How to use Stoicism for the Long Term and Planning Your Future as a Stoic

If you decided that it was time to add Stoicism into your life starting tomorrow, where would be the best place to start? There isn't really a clear starting point, because, like any other philosophy, the path isn't straightforward all the time. your best bet is to learn as much about Stoicism as possible, and then build up from there. Learning new concepts can take some practice, and experimenting with Stoicism a bit and see how it works for you.

Going from an emotional disaster, like many of us, over to a Stoic can be a big adjustment for the brain. You need to actually go through and rewire the way that it thinks. The more you start to hear about Stoicism, the more that you surround yourself with the ideas that come with

Stoicism, and the more that you are able to expose yourself to Stoicism, the easier it is to rewire the brain to behave the way that you want. Even starting out by doing some meditation can make a big difference in how you view the world, how much you can control your anger, and how much you can implement Stoicism into your life.

During this time of education, make a point to put the words that strike you the most into action. If there are some ideas or passages that seem to hit home for you, make sure to add it over to your moral catalog. If you like the idea of gaining control over your emotions, then work on that. If you like the idea of letting go of things that you can't control, then focus your energy on that.

As you learn more about Stoicism, talk to others who use Stoicism, and just get more familiar with Stoicism, you are going to find a lot of things that really strike your interest. Keep these close, and when things get tough, make sure to remind yourself of them. Remember that just hearing these words on a regular basis can be enough to retrain the brain to a new way of thinking. Write the ideas down and then look them over on occasion, and see the difference they can make in your life.

But your whole process into Stoicism shouldn't just be about reading and writing things down the whole time. You need to actually get to work and do some actions to get the benefits of Stoicism in your life. You need to consciously monitor your emotions throughout the day. This isn't going to happen on its own. The brain wants to keep up with its traditional habits and ways of thinking. You have to actually go through and think about your emotions and what you want to happen rather than just letting those emotions happen.

For example, let's say that you are feeling upset or anxious. You can take some time to sit with those thoughts, without reacting, and figure out what is causing them to come in the first place.

What you may not realize here is that your emotions are going to have a direct connection from the brain to the body. When our stomach feels like it is in knots, this is often the brain trying to signal to us that something isn't right at that time. If you can figure out what is causing those feelings, then it is easier for you to make them go away.

Another thing that you can work on when you get started with Stoicism is to not sweat the little things. So many times, the things that really seem to make us the most upset are going to be the littlest things, the ones that don't really matter all that much. The next time that you get stuck in traffic, or you have to listen to your boss drone on during a meeting, allow the emotions to show up, but then invite them to just pass over you.

Yes, at times you are going to feel angry or annoyed at the situation, but these moments are going to pass. Allow yourself to notice the feeling, but then actively decide that you aren't going to assign a value to it at all, and you are not going to react, until the mind has had some turn going over the information.

Again, one of the best things that you can do when you first start with Stoicism, especially if you are prone to lots of anger and stress and frustration, includes meditation. There are many different methods of meditation that you can try out, and all of them can provide you with great results. The goal here, no matter which form of meditation you decide to go with, is to help you learn more about your inner self, to take a break from life, and start to realize that the little things don't matter that much.

You only need to take about fifteen minutes a day, either right away in the morning or right before going to bed. This is enough time to get yourself to calm down, to clear the head, and help you to get in control of what you are feeling. Explore a few different types of meditation, and try a few of them out, to figure out which one you like and want to stick with.

Using Stoicism to plan out your future

Planning your future can be a scary endeavor for some people. They worry that they won't have enough money to pay the bills. They worry that something bad will happen. But most people are just scared about the things that they can't control that may find them when they think about the future. But when you spend all your time being consumed with fear about the future,

Although fate is going to play some role in how your life turns out, your ultimate level of happiness is going to depend on you. This is your chance to make the most out of your life. This may mean that you will need to make some large changes in your life, or it could be as simple as rearranging how you view what is already going on in your life. Before you make the big changes though, explore making some small rearrangements to help you do this in the most effective manner.

For example, when you look at your life, do you see that it is really all that undesirable, or are you just unappreciative or selfish about what you already have in your life? If you find that you are just being selfish, then the only thing that you need to do is learn how to control your thinking and your emotional state, and things will get better. If you look around and notice that your life really isn't desirable, then it is time to make some big changes to your life to add in some more happiness.

If you decide that it is time to make some big changes in your life, then it is time to figure out what you want to do so you can make a plan. Ask yourself some questions like "What could I be doing to live a life that is more fulfilling? What am I doing now that makes me happy? What am I doing to bring meaning to the lives of others?"

While these questions may seem a bit vague in some cases, that is kind of the point. Each of us needs to explore these questions on our own and figure out the answers. Each person is going to come up with different answers and they are likely to change. But it is up to you to figure out the answers to all of these and then come up with the plan that will progress you forward.

At this point, you may be at a loss for how you can get started in Stoicism, and how you can create a plan for improving your own life. Here are some concrete tasks that you can think about to help this plan get started. first, pick out a tangible goal that you want to meet, and then write it down. Stick it along with some of your favorite quotes from Stoicism and leave them in a place where you can find them easily.

Let's say that you had a great idea of going back to school in order to study art. This is something that you always wanted to do, but you listened to your logical mind and went into a career that had more money and more stability. But your current career didn't really help to fill your soul. So, now you are ready to go back to art school and see how that can go for you.

At this point, the question is, how will you do this? Where will you go to school? Will you need help financing the school? How much time can you devote to this? Will you continue working while going to school and how will this affect your overall plan? Do you want to do this on the side or would you want to do this as a full-time career?

Think about all of the little steps that you will need to take in order to help you reach these goals. Then make sure to write these down. Once you have all the different steps in place, you can break them into tiny steps to give you a clear map. Remember that a Stoic mind is often going to be a logical one. It is fine to follow some of the passions that you have in life, but if you just jump in because of the emotions, without thinking through the consequences or the plan of attack, then you are not working as a Stoic. Writing all of this down as a thought-out plan can really help you to make sure you do this the right way.

During this whole process, you may feel like you are being overwhelmed with all of the small details and the hard work that is needed to reach the finish line. You may even start to feel a bit of anxiety and fear as you start to build up your map. This is yet another place where Stoicism can come into play as well. Use the skills that you have learned with Stoicism to take a step back and sit with your emotions.

Think about what is actually causing these emotions. Are you afraid of all the work that you have to do to make it to your goal? Are you scared that you are going to fail? As you are thinking over this goal, think about what the worst case scenario is going to be if you didn't get your art degree? If you have a plan put into place, it's likely that the worst thing you are going to have to deal with is that you stay with your current job and can't pursue your passions. This can be hard, but at least you still have stability and a job, and you can come back and try something else later on.

The motivation to really work on some changes in your life, and to focus on the things that make you happy can be the root of Stoicism. While it does ask you to think through your emotions and have a plan of attack when you are ready to handle any situation out of your control, these can be used to help you see the success that you want out of life. For some people, this can be hard to do. They want to follow their emotions because it is easy, but as we saw in the example above shows that you can listen to your emotions, but you will still use your logical side to help you finish that decision.

You can use these same ideas when it comes to any major decision that you want to follow. Think about the thing that is going to make the biggest difference in your life. What is going to make you happy in the here and now? Once you have that down (and it can be influenced by your emotions), you can use your Stoic mind to come up with a logical plan to actually reach the results that you want for success.

Now that you have given yourself a pep talk, it is time to go through that list that you have made, crossing off the tasks until you have gotten to the goal. Keep the big picture in mind the whole time. And when you actually reach the goal, you will find that you are doing something that you truly love, something that helps you make a good contribution to your community, and you get the benefit of enjoying the fruits of your labor along the way as well.

Planning your future can be tough. There are so many variables that come into play, but often the major reason that we won't sit and think about our future is that we are afraid of what will happen. Yet again, we have decided to let emotions get in the way of our own happiness, and have turned away from using logical thinking to improve our lives. When you start to work more with Stoicism and implementing it into your life with the tools that we discuss in this guidebook, you will find that it can make some great improvements to your future, and can plan out your future much better than you could ever have imagined.

Conclusion

Thank you for making it through to the end of *Stoicism*. Let's hope it was informative and able to provide you with all of the tools you need to achieve your goals whatever they may be.

The next step is to find ways that you are able to implement Stoicism into your own life. Many people have the wrong idea about Stoicism. They think that in order to be a Stoic or follow any of the ideas that come with Stoicism, you need to be void of emotions, cold, and lack sympathy for other people. But, as we explored through this guidebook, Stoics aren't missing out on emotions, they just know how to have emotions without worrying about how those emotions are going to take control over them.

Living a life of Stoicism is a great option to work with. You can take an evaluation of all the emotions you have, and choose whether you would like to express them or take a lot of route. This gives you a ton of freedom, can improve your relationships, helps you get further in life, and is one of the best ways to improve your quality of life.

When you are ready to learn more about Stoicism and how it can benefit your life, make sure to take a look through this guidebook to help you get started.

www.ingramcontent.com/pod-product-compliance
Lightning Source LLC
Chambersburg PA
CBHW071359080526
44587CB00017B/3129